REFUSING TO CRUMBLE

THE DANISH RESISTANCE IN WORLD WAR II

by Michael Burgan

Content Adviser: Malte Möller-Christensen, Guide, The Museum
of the Danish Resistance, Copenhagen, Denmark

Reading Adviser: Alexa L. Sandmann, Ed.D., Professor of Literacy,
College and Graduate School of Education, Health,
and Human Services, Kent State University

COMPASS POINT BOOKS
a capstone imprint

Compass Point Books
151 Good Counsel Drive
P.O. Box 669
Mankato, MN 56002-0669

 This book was manufactured with paper containing
at least 10 percent post-consumer waste.

Editor: Brenda Haugen
Designer: Bobbie Nuytten
Media Researcher: Svetlana Zhurkin
Library Consultant: Kathleen Baxter
Production Specialist: Jane Klenk
Cartographer: XNR Productions, Inc.

Library of Congress Cataloging-in-Publication Data
Burgan, Michael.
  Refusing to crumble: the Danish resistance in World War II / by
Michael Burgan.
      p. cm.——(Taking a stand)
  Includes bibliographical references and index.
  ISBN 978-0-7565-4298-6 (library binding)
  1. World War, 1939–1945—Underground movements—Denmark—Juvenile
literature. 2. Denmark—History—German occupation, 1940–1945—Juvenile
literature. I. Title. II. Series.
  D802.D4B78 2010
  940.53'489—dc22   2009033573

Visit Compass Point Books on the Internet at www.compasspointbooks.com
or e-mail your request to custserv@compasspointbooks.com

IMAGE CREDITS

TABLE OF CONTENTS

CHAPTER ONE

WAR COMES TO DENMARK

I went outside and saw the sky almost blackened by German planes. Instead of dropping bombs they dropped leaflets. I grabbed one. ... They told us not to resist or there would be terrible consequences. That was the beginning.

Knud Dyby, member of the Danish resistance

Jørgen Kieler was eager to continue his college studies in Copenhagen, the capital of Denmark. The 20-year-old wanted to be a doctor, like his father, and he had already studied in Great Britain and Germany. As he prepared for courses in August 1939, Kieler and the rest of the world didn't realize that those two nations would soon be at war. The global conflict would bring painful changes to Denmark—and great personal challenges for Kieler.

Blitzkrieg

Before dawn on September 1, 1939, a German battleship's guns roared to life, sending shells toward Polish troops stationed near Danzig, Poland. Across Poland, residents soon saw German planes overhead. Then, as the sun began to rise, German troops and tanks rushed across the Polish border. As the Germans advanced across the countryside, civilians fled or sought shelter, while Polish troops defended their homeland from the more powerful foe. Many fell, wounded or dead, victims of what the Germans called *blitzkrieg*—"lightning war." World War II had begun.

Germany's leader, Adolf Hitler, had been

Without a formal declaration of war, the Germans invaded Poland.

planning the war for years. Hitler led the Nazi Party. He and his fellow Nazis had taken control of the German government in 1933. After World War I (1914–1918), the winning countries had forced a defeated Germany to give up some of its land. France, Great Britain, the United States, and the other Allies also had made Germany destroy its weapons. Germany's weakened state had angered Hitler, who sought to rebuild his country's military and spread its power.

Adolf Hitler ruled Germany with a heavy hand.

Hitler blamed most of Germany's problems on Jews. He wrongly believed that their business dealings gave them power over much of the world. Jews became the focus of his hatred. He took away their legal rights and began sending them to concentration camps. Eventually Hitler and the Nazis would launch a plan to kill all the Jews in Europe. The Nazis also detested Slavs, the people of Poland, Russia, and other Eastern European countries. Hitler thought the Germans were a "master race," entitled to control most of Europe. The invasion of Poland was Hitler's first step toward achieving that goal.

Denmark and Germany

Jørgen Kieler knew the war would affect Denmark in some way. His country shared a border with Germany and had strong business ties with the Nazis' main enemy, Great Britain. In southern Denmark, some families had roots in Germany, and they supported good relations with the country. Yet many Danes remembered the wars their country had fought against Germany during the 19th century. In the end, Germany had won control of some Danish lands. Many Danes still disliked and feared the Germans because of that loss.

During World War I, Denmark had been neutral. After the 1939 German invasion of Poland, the Danes again asserted their neutrality. Still the Danes knew they would have no way to defend themselves if Hitler attacked them. Denmark's military was too small to stop the massive German forces.

In November 1939, fighting erupted in the eastern part of

Scandinavia. With Germany's agreement, the Soviet Union invaded

Finland. Several thousand Danes rushed to help the Finns fight

their invaders. Kieler was one of the volunteers. But when he went to sign up, Kieler discovered he needed to get military training before he could join the war. His desire to fight evil, however, never weakened, and the years to come would give him his chance.

The Invasion

Early on April 9, 1940, the first of about 38,000 German soldiers entered Denmark. They came by land into Jutland, the southern part of Denmark. Sixteen Danish soldiers and border police-men died in the invasion. German paratroops landed in northern Jutland, and other German forces came by ship. In Copenhagen German planes destroyed the Danish air force.

German forces took control of key government buildings in Copen-hagen. As they approached the palace, shots came from almost every direction as the guards tried to defend their beloved King Christian X. Soon Denmark's leaders received a message from the Germans: If the Danes did not stop fighting, the Germans would bomb Copen-hagen. The government agreed to the Germans' demands.

Some Danes seemed to welcome the Germans. Denmark even

had a few Nazis of its own. They and Germans living in Denmark had helped guide the invaders through the country. Most Danes, however, were stunned and saddened by the invasion.

Germany in Control

As the invasion went on, the Germans said King Christian could keep his throne. The Danish government would operate as it had before. The Nazis, though, did bring in the Schutzstaffel, their own special security force. By torturing and killing innocent people, the SS created terror wherever it went. The SS troops were there to make sure the Danes did what they were told. This included providing Germany with food and supplies for its war effort. Yet for most Danes, life remained normal and the Germans treated them fairly well—for a time.

King Christian X remained the Danish monarch, but the Germans were in control.

CHAPTER TWO

FIRST STEPS

Our people have lost some of the most precious rights guaranteed under the [Danish] Constitution. They have lost their liberty ... we are no longer masters in our own house ... but I can tell you that every Dane of every party—rich or poor, young or old—is hoping and praying that the cause of justice will win and that a free and independent Denmark will be re-established.

Henrik Kauffmann, Danish minister to the United States

Henrik Kauffmann enjoyed his job as Denmark's top diplomat in the United States. On April 9, 1940, he was traveling in South Carolina when he received devastating news—his homeland was under attack by the Germans.

Kauffmann cut short his trip and rushed back to Washington, D.C., to meet with President Franklin D. Roosevelt. Kauffmann refused to accept German control of his government, and Roosevelt agreed to recognize him as the official Danish diplomat in the United States.

A Growing War

On the day of the Danish invasion, the Germans also attacked Norway. Later they stormed through the Netherlands and Belgium. By June 1940, they also controlled France.

Many Danish leaders believed Germany would achieve all of

its aims and win the war. They decided it made sense to remain on good terms with the Nazis and help them in Denmark. This angered Danes who hated their loss of freedom and the Nazis' bloody tactics in other countries.

The day after France formally surrendered, Hitler (center) toured some of the sites, including the Eiffel Tower in Paris.

These Danes looked for ways to resist German occupation.

Even before the German victories in France and elsewhere, some Danes showed they would not give in easily to German control. As news of the April 9 invasion spread, several hundred Danish merchant ships at sea began to head to British and other Allied ports. The sailors did not want the Germans to have control of the ships. About 5,000 of the sailors eventually served in Allied navies during the war.

Taking Action

In July 1940, Danes living in London met to discuss volunteering to fight for Great Britain. That country was the only one left in Western Europe that could possibly defeat Germany. As the war went on, other Danes left Denmark for Great Britain to join the war effort.

The British were already taking their own steps to help Denmark and other occupied nations. The government created a new department called the Special Operations Executive. The SOE trained Europeans to carry out sabotage in their occupied homelands.

Ignoring German orders, the crew of a Danish ship unloaded its cargo in Great Britain.

This included destroying trains carrying German troops and blowing up factories making supplies for the Germans. The agents also collected intelligence about German military activities. The SOE soon set up a group in England to train Danes who were eager to help their country resist the Germans.

As part of their training, the Danish SOE agents learned how to operate wireless radio sets. The radios sent messages back and forth between two locations. The resistance fighters needed radios to contact planes bringing supplies to Denmark. The radio operators would tell the planes where and when to drop the supplies. The Danes also learned how to parachute, so they could jump from British planes into Denmark. Resistance fighters were taught how to make bombs and shoot guns.

The British and Danes began working together in Sweden, too.

The Germans did not invade that country, and Danes could easily travel there by boat. Once in Stockholm, the Swedish capital, they could meet with British officials there to discuss resistance efforts or travel on to London to train as resistance fighters.

Words and Protests

When the occupation began, the Germans limited freedom of the press. The Danes still controlled newspapers and radio stations, but they knew they could not say anything to upset the Germans. To learn about events outside Denmark, Danes listened to the British Broadcasting Corporation. The BBC offered programs in Danish. As the resistance grew, Britain's Special Operations Executive used these broadcasts to send secret codes to their agents in Denmark.

Some Danes began to create "underground" (illegal) newspapers. The underground press aimed to educate the Danes about the war and create more resistance against the Germans. A few of the newspapers had first appeared in 1940. Most were published by members of the Communist Party. The Communists called for the government to own all factories and businesses. They strongly opposed Nazi beliefs. The Communists were not a major political party in Denmark. Few Danes supported the Communist goal of giving the government greater control over the economy. Yet the Communists led some of the first resistance efforts.

In June 1941, Germany invaded the Soviet Union, which was communist. In November the Germans pressured the Danish government to join the Anti-Comintern Pact. Germany and Japan had created this agreement in 1936 to fight communism and their common enemy—the Soviet Union. The Danish government agreed to join them and signed the pact, which sparked protests in Copenhagen. The protesters didn't support the Soviet Union, but they didn't want Denmark to give in-again—to the Germans.

Germany's motorized infantry advanced into Ukraine as it invaded the Soviet Union.

BUILDING ANGER

In his autobiography, Jørgen Kieler wrote about his experience at the rally of people protesting the Anti-Comintern Pact:

There was a mood of revolt and people were enthusiastic as we marched along. ... 'Sing on, students!' was what people were calling to us. We tried, but we were not particularly good at singing. And we were also busy looking out in case we spotted any Germans, whose interference we expected. But we were only confronted by the Danish police. They swung their [clubs] without, however, doing much damage. ... The Anti-Comintern protest demonstration marked the start of cooperation by a number of students in organized resistance against occupation and collaboration.

CHAPTER THREE

ACTIVE RESISTANCE AT LAST

We should never forget, that one cannot have anything [free] in this world. ... We must help, ourselves. ... It must not be, that Denmark is missing in the common fight against the whole world's tyrants. ... It is a definite and consistent resistance against the German violations, [that] the times demand of each one of us. ... We must face the risk.

Christmas Møller, writing in the underground newspaper *Free Denmark*

Parachutes strapped to their backs, Carl Johan Bruhn and Mogens Hammer heard the roar of the engines powering their Wellington bomber. The aircraft was flying over the North Sea from England to Denmark. Bruhn had been studying medicine in England when World War II began. He soon began working with the Special

Operations Executive. The British chose him to lead an effort to contact resistance groups in Denmark. Hammer was trained to operate the radio Bruhn would use in Denmark to contact England.

On the night of December 27, 1941, the Wellington approached the small Danish town of Haslev. Bruhn and Hammer waited for the signal to jump. They would be making a blind drop, meaning that no one would be waiting for them on the ground. They had the name of a contact and code words that would prove to Danish resistance members that they really were part of the SOE.

In the dark winter night, Bruhn and Hammer stepped out of the plane, beginning their fall. As he neared the ground, Bruhn saw that something was wrong. The cord that opened his chute was supposed to be attached to the plane. At the right distance from the plane, the cord would snap open the chute. But the chute cord was not attached. Hammer's parachute opened, but Bruhn's did not. Bruhn crashed to the ground, dying instantly. Hammer landed safely, but his radio was destroyed. He set out alone for Copenhagen. He reached the city, but in the months that followed, a secret police force in the SS called the Gestapo searched for him. Hammer finally had to row to safety in a kayak, reaching Sweden.

By January 1, the British knew the first resistance drop had ended badly. But the deadly results did not stop the effort to connect the SOE with the growing Danish resistance movement. More parachutists followed, landing safely and beginning their resistance efforts. The British, though, had few planes available to bring resistance members and their supplies to Denmark. The British were more focused on fighting the Germans directly. Through 1942 the Danes could only carry out small acts of sabotage and defiance. But each act stirred the hope that more would follow.

Students Take Charge

Arne Sejr disliked his government's official response to the German invasion. So the 17-year-old Dane began his own personal resistance

The resistance sabotaged a German truck in Copenhagen.

to the occupation. Working quickly on a typewriter, he wrote "Ten Commandments for Danes"—a list of actions he thought they should take against the Germans. One was: "You must destroy important machines and gear, you must destroy everything useful to the Germans, you must deal with traitors as they deserve." Then, at night, he crept through the empty streets, pushing copies of his document through the mail slots of political and business leaders in his hometown.

By 1942 Sejr was attending a university in Copenhagen. He was one of the leaders of the Students' Information Service. The group secretly published books and newspapers for the resistance.

One important Dane who worked with the students was Christmas Møller. A former government official, he refused to work with the Germans, and they forced him out of his job. Møller then provided secret government documents to Sejr and the student publishers. In April 1942, Møller and his family sneaked out of Denmark into Sweden and flew to London. Møller began to deliver radio addresses on the BBC. His voice became a source of comfort and pride to the Danes, as he urged them to resist the Germans. Møller also wrote for a new underground paper, *Free Denmark*. The most important of the papers, *Free Denmark* first appeared on April 9, 1942, the second anniversary of the invasion.

An article in *Free Denmark* dealt with what resistance members felt was a Danish government too willing to accommodate the Germans.

Frit Danmark

Nr. 9   Udgivet af en Kreds af Danske   Dec. 1942

Den tyske Lydregering i Danmark

Ministeriet Scavenius' Tiltræden blev i brede Kredse modtaget med en vis Lettelse. Det kan ikke nytte at nægte det. Den Uges Forhandlinger, som gik forud, indeholdt saa mange ildevarslende Episo-

tryk for af Danskhed, af Selvstændighed og af Stolthed — og det var ikke stort —, fejede Hr. Ribbentrops Tillidsmand, Erik Scavenius, bort med en Haandbevægelse og nøjedes med at nagle Rigsdagen — og ikke mindst Knud Kristensen Manden der

The paper did not call for sabotage against the Germans, but it encouraged Danes to resist in less violent ways. Resistance leaders knew the Danes still needed more money and members to carry out active resistance.

The Churchill Club

The lack of money, however, meant nothing to Knud and Jens Pedersen. Along with some other boys, the brothers used a toy printing press to publish their own underground paper. At other times, they painted anti-German messages on walls, encouraging resistance to the Germans. Together the boys, ranging in age from 14 to 18, were known as the Churchill Club, named after British Prime Minister Winston Churchill, who was leading England in its war against Germany. The Pedersen brothers formed the first club in the town of Odense and another when they moved to Aalborg. Their motto was: "If you older folk will do nothing, we will have to do something instead!"

The boys quickly turned from words to more daring action. They stole German soldiers' guns, waiting until most of them had left their barracks. Reaching through open windows, they grabbed rifles nearby. The guns would help protect the boys as they carried out sabotage against the Germans.

The Churchill Club seemed to come to an end in May 1942, when Knud Pedersen was caught stealing a pistol. He and other members were arrested. But even in jail they kept carrying out sabotage. Friends brought them metal files, which they used to saw through the bars of their cells. The jailers did not watch the boys closely, and at night several were able to sneak out and destroy more property, sneaking back in before they were missed. A few weeks later, though, the older members were sentenced to prison, and the club came to an end.

But new resistance efforts began. In July a group of Communists known as Kopa damaged a wharf in Copenhagen. The group soon grew to include non-Communists and was renamed Bopa. It divided its members into sections, and it produced "The Saboteur's Cookbook," a 100-page guide explaining how to make bombs and carry out attacks. Bopa focused on factories in Copenhagen that made war supplies for the Nazis.

A New Resistance Leader

On the night of March 12, 1943, a Danish man hanging from a parachute drifted down onto Fyn, an island in the center of Denmark. The parachutist, Flemming Muus, had been in Africa when Germany invaded Denmark. Full of anger and sadness about the news, Muus had taken a crude canoe and set out for England, rowing along the coast of West Africa. For almost two weeks, the sun had burned down on him, and his body had grown weaker, but he had been determined to get to his goal. Finally reaching England, he had joined the SOE. He had become the group's leader in Denmark—but he had to get there first.

Flemming Muus and Varinka Wichfield risked their lives to help the Danish resistance.

To reach Copenhagen from Fyn, Muus needed to take a ferry. Approaching the boat, he saw about

10 armed German soldiers checking everyone's documents. Muus was using a fake name, "Mr. Miller." As Muus later recalled, the Germans were "ready to arrest anyone who seemed the least bit suspicious. I went past them with my heart in my mouth." Despite his fear, Muus safely passed the Germans and took the ferry to Copenhagen.

As the SOE leader, Muus wanted Denmark to actively take the side of the Allies against the Germans. For this to happen, the Danish government had to fall, since it was still following Germany's orders. Muus and the SOE hoped increased protests and sabotage would bring down the government.

An Unlikely Helper

Soon after he arrived, Muus met an unlikely member of the growing resistance movement, Monica Wichfeld. A mother of three in her mid 40s who had been born into a wealthy British family, she had married a Dane named Jørgen Wichfeld. The Wichfelds had returned to Denmark after the start of the war. The German occupation angered Monica Wichfeld. Now both her homeland of Great Britain and her adopted home were under Nazi threat.

In 1942 Wichfeld learned that a member of the resistance was renting a cottage on her family's country estate. The man at first was suspicious of her. Many wealthy Danes quietly supported the Germans.

Monica Wichfeld's large estate, called Engestofte, included many places where she could hide supplies for the resistance.

The occupation had barely affected their lives, and some made money supplying the Germans with food and supplies. But Wichfeld assured him she strongly opposed the Nazis. Soon she was giving the tenant money she had collected from friends to support underground newspapers.

The next year, Wichfeld contacted local resistance leaders and offered to hide members of the resistance in her home when they learned that the Gestapo knew about their activities. They needed "safe houses" where they could hide before escaping to Sweden. The Wichfeld home was so large that Wichfeld could take in the resistance members without the rest of her family knowing. She did all her resistance work secretly; only her daughter Varinka knew about her work.

Meeting with Flemming Muus, Wichfeld told him the SOE could drop supplies and men at the fields near her home. Muus put her in charge of receiving the drops and hiding the SOE agents.

Wichfeld recruited people to help her. Word spread through a nearby town that she could arrange for training so young men could help the resistance. Varinka helped her mother, and eventually she became Muus' assistant.

In the months that followed, Wichfeld took action herself. Some nights she picked up bags of explosives dropped by the SOE. She loaded them into the family's small rowboat and crossed a lake on the estate to bury the explosives in a safe place. She made the trip so many times that her hands became hardened with calluses from clutching the oars. But nothing could stop her from carrying out this work—except the Germans themselves.

A Successful Strike

With the help of the Wichfelds and others, Muus and his men carried out a major attack in August 1943. Danish workers were turning the Forum, the largest public hall in Copenhagen, into barracks for German troops. One day when the workers were on their lunch break, a delivery boy rode his bike to the Forum. He carried a wooden box like the ones used to carry bottles of beer. But inside this box was 100 pounds (45 kilograms) of explosives. Two resistance members dressed as workers carried the box into the empty building,

The Forum was used to house German soldiers who were on leave from Norway.

placed the explosives in several spots, lit the fuses, and left. Suddenly the quiet was broken by massive blasts. The devastating attack on the Forum came after hundreds of smaller acts of sabotage across the country.

By the summer of 1943, World War II had turned in favor of the Allies. The growing Allied success made more Danes willing to resist the Germans and to become part of the Allies themselves. But Adolf Hitler issued a warning: If the Danes would not stop the sabotage, the Germans would.

Risks and Assistance

Even before the Forum blast, resistance members who were caught were often sent to concentration camps. But in some cases, the Germans simply executed them.

In May 1943, the Germans sentenced saboteur Hans Petersen to death. In Copenhagen the news angered Jørgen Kieler. Still in college, Kieler juggled his studying with work for the underground press. After hearing about Petersen's execution, Kieler was ready to take even more daring actions.

Danes overturned a police van during a riot in Odense.

In June he and several friends made plans to strike a building that housed electrical equipment. His little group was not in contact with the SOE. They had to steal the simple explosives they used. The attack, he later wrote, was "not particularly successful." Despite the failure, Kieler soon tried again, with slightly more success. Later he would lead an important resistance group.

Throughout 1943 the number of sabotage attacks grew tremendously. In all of 1941, the Danes had carried out 19 attacks.

In just July 1943, there were 93. By now the resistance was getting help from a new group of Danes: the police. A growing number of police officers actively helped the resistance, while others ignored their actions.

Knud Dyby was one of the helpful officers. He had been living in Copenhagen when the Germans had invaded, and he decided to join the police force. One of his jobs was preventing Danes from attacking Germans. But as the occupation dragged on, Dyby and other officers increasingly supported the resistance. They sometimes knew about planned sabotage and went to the target sites before-hand. Danish companies often hired guards to protect factories and railways from sabotage. With his gun drawn, Dyby persuaded the guards to leave or look away, so the sabotage could take place.

The various acts of sabotage and resistance were adding up. The Germans grew angrier with the Danes and their government. Finally, in August 1943, a new crisis erupted. The Danes were about to see Hitler's anger and Nazi brutality as they never had before: firsthand.

CHAPTER FOUR

THE GERMANS TAKE CONTROL

The captain ... said something like this: "In five minutes, the Hvidbjørnen [naval ship] will be blown up. We can look our fellow Danes straight in the eye when we get home. We have done our duty."

Svend Kieler, a Danish sailor aboard the *Hvidbjørnen*, which the captain blew up rather than turn it over to the Germans

Werner Best returned to Germany to discuss the continuing resistance in Denmark with Nazi leaders. Since fall 1942, he had been the German representative in Copenhagen. Although a high-ranking SS officer, Best had tried to create good relations with Danish officials to keep the supply of food and other goods flowing from Denmark to Germany. Now, though, with the sabotage continuing,

Hitler was not willing to listen to Best's explanations. Hitler had a list of demands for the Danes. They included a nightly curfew, tighter restrictions on newspapers, and execution of all saboteurs.

Best took the demands to Denmark and gave Danish officials less than eight hours to respond. Their answer was short and direct: They would not accept Hitler's demands. The Danish government dissolved itself. The cooperation with the Germans stopped.

The Nazis Take Over

The explosion at Copenhagen's Forum wasn't the only act that had angered the Nazis. Throughout August workers had gone on strike across Denmark, refusing to work in factories that made goods for the Germans. People also had taken to the streets in protest. The Nazis responded to the growing resistance by picking out people at random for arrests or beatings. The news of the Danes' activities led to the demands that Best brought with him from Berlin.

The Danish refusal came August 28, 1943. The next morning, the Germans declared a state of emergency in Denmark. They were now in control of the country. German troops began attacking

Danish military sites. The Danes had been ordered not to resist, but a few did, and the Germans killed 17 of them. The Germans tried to seize Danish naval ships as well. Most of the captains destroyed their ships or sailed to Sweden rather than let the Germans take them.

Germans reacted with violence to the August 1943 strikes that broke out across Denmark.

The Nazis and the Jews

During World War II, Hitler's anti-Semitism caused great trouble for most of the Jews in Europe. Starting in Germany and then in the lands he conquered, Hitler had Jews sent to concentration camps. Some of these places became death camps, where Jews were killed by the thousands.

Hitler called the killing of the Jews the "Final Solution." He thought he was solving the "problem" of Jews' harming Germany.

The mass killings came to be known as the Holocaust.

The Nazis had help as they carried out Hitler's plans. Anti-Semitism existed in most parts of the world. Many Europeans either helped the Germans get rid of the local Jews or at least did not resist. The Danes were different. Fewer than 8,000 Jews lived in Denmark in 1943, but non-Jewish Danes would not ignore them or let them die. And helping the Jews was another way to show their resistance to the occupation.

The First Steps

Georg Duckwitz was a German working for Werner Best in Denmark. He had lived there before the war and had good relations with many Danes. Duckwitz would play an important role in the next major act of Danish resistance.

Early in September 1943, Duckwitz learned from Best that the Nazis planned to send Danish Jews to concentration camps. Both men opposed the idea, fearing it would strain relations between Germans and Danes. Best, however, was not going to disobey an order, while Duckwitz was ready to take action to stop the deportation plan.

Duckwitz told the Swedish government that it should prepare to receive Danish Jews who would be escaping the Nazis. The Swedes agreed. Then Duckwitz met with German coast guard commanders who patrolled Danish waters. He persuaded them to keep their ships in dock when the Nazi deporta-

Risking his own life, Georg Duckwitz warned of the planned roundup of Denmark's Jews.

tion started. That way Danish fishing boats could safely carry Jews to Sweden.

Duckwitz sent word to Jewish leaders in Denmark about the coming deportation, scheduled for the beginning of October. He contacted Danish friends with ties to political leaders. The word began to spread, and Jews soon realized they needed to hide or leave the country.

A Nation Responds

The united Danish effort to save the Jews has been called one of the greatest acts of moral courage during the war. Clergy and university students spoke out against the deportation. Schools and hospitals hid Jews. Across Denmark strangers helped strangers, offering the fleeing Jews food, places to sleep, or help in finding boats.

As the refugees sought shelter and made their way to the boats, they and the Danes who helped them knew they faced danger. Although the German naval commanders had agreed not to take action, the SS and Gestapo would try to keep the Jews from leaving if they could. People aiding them could be arrested.

Escape by Sea

The fishing fleet of Denmark provided the last step to freedom for Denmark's Jews. In good weather, depending on where a boat left Denmark, a trip to Sweden could take just an hour. In stormy seas, though, small fishing boats could drift for hours on the water, the cramped passengers inside fighting back nausea. Adding to the danger, mines sometimes rode on the waves. Hitting one of the floating explosives would blow a small boat into pieces and probably kill everyone aboard.

On October 1, the Germans began to knock on the doors of Jewish homes. Jews who had refused to flee were dragged into cars or vans, the first stage of the frightening trip to the concentration camps. But as the searching went on, the Nazis could find only a few hundred Jews. The rest either were hiding or had already escaped. By the end of October, the Danes had taken about 7,200 Jews

Danish fishing boats carrying Jewish refugees were met by Swedish vessels when they entered Swedish waters.

to Sweden. About 1,000 of them were children under the age of 10. The Danes used more than 300 boats, mostly small fishing boats, to carry their special cargo. Once in Sweden, the Jews received food and shelter. Most remained there as refugees for the rest of the war.

By this time, leaders from various resistance groups and political parties had formed the Freedom Council. Operating in secret, this group coordinated all resistance efforts in Denmark. With the Jews safely evacuated, the council focused on getting more help from the Allies and carrying out more sabotage. They had beaten the Nazis by spoiling their plan to kill Danish Jews. Now the Danes had to win back their freedom.

A rescued Jewish refugee is helped off a Danish fishing boat during the German occupation of Denmark.

CHAPTER FIVE

THE RESISTANCE GROWS

Comrades, you must not feel sad. You know why we have fought, and it is for Denmark we die.

Sven Johannesen, who was executed by the Germans
for his resistance activities

On a December night in 1943, three Danish resistance members sat in a small house in Aarhus, Denmark. Suddenly the house was swarming with armed Gestapo agents. The Danes had guns. They also had poison pills, which many agents carried in case they were caught. They thought it was better to die than risk being tortured and reveal information that would harm resistance operations. But these three men did not take their pills or try to shoot their way to freedom. Instead they went quietly with the Germans, adding to the almost 600 people the Gestapo had arrested that year. The three men talked rather than face torture. Other resistance members paid the price for their cowardice.

Prison

Still asleep on a cold January morning, Monica Wichfeld did not hear the two armed Gestapo agents until they stormed into her room. She woke to see the men standing over her. They told her to get dressed and prepare for a long trip.

The men arrested in Aarhus had given the Germans the names of Monica Wichfeld, Flemming Muus, and several dozen other resistance members. Muus had avoided arrest, but Wichfeld was not so lucky. The Germans threw her into jail. In May 1944, she was sentenced to die. Wichfeld would have been the first woman executed in Denmark in centuries, but the Germans later changed their minds and sent her to a concentration camp instead. She was one of several hundred resistance members sent to the camps.

Holger Danske 2

The threat of arrest or torture didn't stop the activities of a group called Holger Danske. The group's

name came from the hero of a Danish folktale. Holger Danske was said to be so huge that people had to climb up a ladder to reach his shoulders. More important, the legendary giant had helped defend Denmark from a foreign invasion. When some of the leaders of the Holger Danske resistance group were forced to flee to Sweden, a new group, called Holger Danske 2, soon formed. Jørgen Kieler and his friends played an important part in HD2.

From the end of October 1943 through February 1944, Kieler's branch of HD2 carried out 26 acts of sabotage. SOE agents supplied the group with explosives and guns. Not all the attacks worked as planned, but sometimes the groups had spectacular success. They used bombs to start destructive fires inside several factories that made goods for the Germans.

The missions, though, were always risky, as Kieler learned in February 1944. He and several other HD2 members were sent to blow up factories in southern Denmark. Soon after they reached their second target, the HD2 group was spotted, and the men began to run. The Danes were soon caught. Kieler went to jail, faced a trial, and ended up in a German concentration camp.

The General Strike

As 1944 went on, more Danes were willing to resist, especially after June 6. On that day, D-Day, the first of 150,000 U.S., British, and Canadian troops swarmed onto beaches in northwest France. The D-Day attack was meant to drive the Germans out of France and the other lands they occupied in Western Europe. At the same time, Soviet troops were continuing to push the Germans out of Eastern Europe. Most people now saw that the Germans could not win the war.

After D-Day the Allies gave more aid to the Danish resistance, and the Freedom Council and the SOE committed more acts of sabotage. On June 22, resistance members stole weapons from a Copenhagen arms factory and then blew it up. The Germans responded by executing eight Danes the next day.

The Germans also again laid down a curfew. In response workers at the Copenhagen shipyard refused to work full days. Soon other workers in the city were also on strike. They gathered in the streets by the hundreds. To show their anger, they turned over streetcars and blocked streets, setting fire to mattresses, paper, and anything else that would burn. Armed Germans drove through the city, firing at anyone they saw. Six Danes were killed during the riot as they protested

The Riffel Syndikat factory, which produced machine guns for Germany, was destoyed by sabotage.

the ongoing occupation, and dozens were wounded by German bullets. The number of casualties rose in the days that followed.

By July 1, the strikes and protests had spread across Copenhagen. Offices and businesses closed, and the telephone system was shut down. Strikes also began outside the city. The countrywide resistance was called the General Strike. The Germans responded by sending troops that had been based outside the city into Copenhagen. The Germans shut off water and electricity and halted the delivery of food. They hoped these measures would force the Danes to give in. Instead the air was soon filled with sharp smell of burning lumber, ripped from buildings the Nazis had used as offices.

German officials called in Georg Duckwitz to try to deal with the Danes. He talked with the Freedom Council, which demanded that all the troops leave Copenhagen. The council also wanted the Germans to restore food, water, and public services. The Germans agreed to remove the troops and consider ending the curfew. The Freedom Council accepted this and called an end to the strike.

The General Strike seemed to be a victory for the resistance. Still some Nazis wanted to prove their power over Denmark. The terror

TELLING THE WORLD

As the General Strike went on, reporters based in Stockholm sent word to newspapers in the United States and elsewhere. On July 2, 1944, *The New York Times* reported:

> *German troops with tanks and machine guns occupied strategic points in the Danish capital, such as the railroad station, the town hall and bridges linking Copenhagen with Amager, as well as blocking all exits from the city. ... The Germans have [taken over] all private automobiles and trucks to bring troops into the capital. This has become necessary because the railroads have been [shut down] by the strike. ... Thousands of inhabitants have attempted to flee the city on bicycle or by horse-drawn carriages since automobiles are not to be found. ... The battle on the Copenhagen streets continued throughout the night with great fury.*

attacks against the Danes continued. And the Germans took yet another step toward limiting the power of Danes to help the resistance.

End of the Police

Police officer Knud Dyby was off duty September 19, but he responded when he heard air raid sirens wail all across Copenhagen. As he rode his bike toward the police station, he saw people duck indoors while drivers quickly stopped their cars so they too could take shelter. Dyby noticed, however, that the sky was quiet—no planes flew overhead, no German artillery boomed. Something was different about this "air raid."

Dyby sooned learned what it was.

A rifle shot whizzed close to his head, nearly knocking off his cap. Approaching the station, he saw German troops forcing police officers into trucks. Werner Best knew that many Danish police and border guards had been helping the resistance, so he had ordered their arrest. From then on, German soldiers and the Gestapo would enforce Nazi orders, while many of the former Danish police officers would sit in German prisons.

SS agents dressed as civilians had sneaked guns into the country's police stations to begin the mass arrests. On the streets, German soldiers tracked down police officers on patrol. Since Dyby was not in uniform, he managed to slip away. He decided to do even more to help the resistance.

Dyby soon arranged for more boats to travel between Denmark and Sweden. The boats carried supplies and important military information as well as people.

As 1945 began, Dyby and the rest of the Danish resistance continued their work. Their confidence was growing, because an Allied victory seemed certain, even though the fighting dragged on in Europe. Yet the Danes still had more to do in their struggle against Germany.

CHAPTER SIX

VICTORY AND FREEDOM

We passed a young German soldier standing guard on the bridge. ... He stood there with his submachine, not knowing whether to laugh or cry, run or shoot. A fellow from the crowd came up and patted him on the back. "Don't worry, now you can go home," he said.

Anne Ipsen, describing events after Germany agreed to leave Denmark

Ruth Philipsen sat in a chair as two Gestapo agents looked down at her. Philipsen, a resistance member, was being held in the Gestapo office in Aarhus, in central Jutland. The area was a center for Danish resistance, and the Germans were arresting more members there, then using torture to get names and other information. But even after 25 days in jail and repeated questioning, Philipsen never revealed what they wanted.

As the questioning went on this time, she heard a buzzing sound that seemed to be coming from an approaching plane, but not one she had heard before. The sound grew louder. Then she heard booms as bombs began falling on the building. Suddenly a bomb made a direct hit on the office. Philipsen was covered with chunks of wall and ceiling. She crawled out of the wreckage, bleeding and shaking, but alive. The Gestapo agents were dead. She scrambled through the rubble and fled the building.

Blow for Blow

Three waves of small British planes called Mosquitoes carried out the October 31, 1944, attack on the Aarhus Gestapo building. The Danish resistance had called for the attack, hoping to slow the Germans' increasing reprisals against the Danes. The office contained files on resistance members, with information turned over by collaborators or gathered through torture. The raid destroyed the building and the files and killed about 150 Gestapo agents.

In the months after D-Day, the Germans had increased their efforts to arrest Danish resistance members and take their weapons and supplies. A December 1944 report told Hitler and his aides that the Germans had arrested 800 people in Denmark since August 1, had killed 35 resistance members, and had captured several tons of weapons and explosives. But the Allies managed to deliver several hundred tons of new supplies, by both sea and air. And more Danes were taking part in sabotage than ever before.

With each Danish blow, the Germans struck back. Gangs of pro-German Danes randomly killed one civilian for every German soldier killed. The Gestapo did not even bother arresting some suspected resistance members. Instead they just killed them.

Soon after the Aarhus raid, the Freedom Council asked the British to bomb the Gestapo headquarters in Copenhagen. After the first raid, the Nazis had feared an attack there, so they had moved many prisoners to the top part

Great Britain's Royal Air Force dropped supplies by parachute into Denmark.

of the building. They assumed the British would not kill important resistance members. Once again the British carefully planned the mission for its Mosquitoes. This time the pilots directed their bombs at the lower floors of the building. Although six Danes were killed, 26 resistance prisoners managed to escape the bomb blasts. But the attack was not a total success. Several planes mistakenly bombed a school, killing 106 people. A few weeks later, the British successfully bombed a third Gestapo headquarters.

The End of German Rule

At about the time of the last raid on the Gestapo, Jørgen Kieler and other captured Danish resistance members received good news— they were being released. Count Folke Bernadotte of Sweden had talked with Nazi officials about freeing Danes and Norwegians held in concentration camps. The Nazis agreed to let the prisoners go to Sweden. Dozens of buses traveled to the camps and picked up 15,000 prisoners, including Danish Jews.

The Germans' decision to free Kieler and the others came as the war was ending. By mid-April the Allies had entered Germany from both the east and the west. Soviet troops were racing toward Berlin, the capital of Germany. By this time, thousands of German refugees had settled in Denmark to escape the war.

On April 30, 1945, Hitler killed himself. Hitler's successor, Karl Dönitz, met with the leaders of the occupation in Denmark to discuss what to do there. Dönitz decided to surrender all the German forces in Denmark, the Netherlands, and part of Germany. The other German forces would keep fighting.

On May 4, the Germans told the Allies they would leave Denmark. Resistance members who had been in England or Sweden came back to Denmark. They included Flemming Muus and Varinka Wichfeld, who was now Muus' wife. Monica Wichfeld, however, never saw Denmark again. She had died while in prison in Germany. Knud Dyby, meanwhile, made his last boat trip as a resistance member, carrying reporters

Buses transported concentration camp prisoners back to Denmark in 1945.

from Sweden to Copenhagen. Danish Jews who had found safety in Sweden also began to return home.

Healing From the Pain

With the Allied liberation, King Christian X once again took his throne. The Danes created a new government. It included previous government leaders and important members of the Freedom Council.

In the first few days after the German forces left, resistance members acted as the police. They arrested Gestapo agents and other Germans, as well as Danes who had collaborated with the Nazis. In all, the new government arrested about 20,000 people. Under the new government, 78 collaborators and Germans received death sentences, although not all of them were executed. In general the government tried to limit violence against collaborators and to treat them fairly.

As the years went by, many Danes said little about the war years. Today, though, the world knows more about the bravery Danes showed during World War II. Their resistance effort was unparalleled in the war against Adolf Hitler and the Nazis.

TIMELINE

April 9, 1940
Germany occupies Denmark

April 9, 1942
First appearance of *Free Denmark*, the most important underground newspaper during the war

August 29, 1943
Germany declares a state of emergency in Denmark and tightens its control

December 27, 1941
The British Special Operations Executive sends the first trained Danish resistance members into Denmark

August 24, 1943
SOE members blow up the Forum, Copenhagen's largest public hall

September–October 1943
Danes unite to help about 7,000 Jews flee Denmark for Sweden

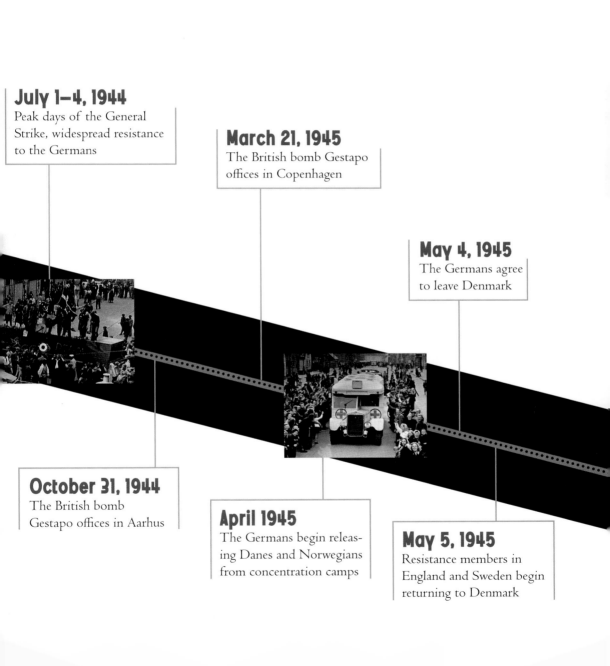

July 1–4, 1944
Peak days of the General Strike, widespread resistance to the Germans

March 21, 1945
The British bomb Gestapo offices in Copenhagen

May 4, 1945
The Germans agree to leave Denmark

October 31, 1944
The British bomb Gestapo offices in Aarhus

April 1945
The Germans begin releasing Danes and Norwegians from concentration camps

May 5, 1945
Resistance members in England and Sweden begin returning to Denmark

GLOSSARY

Allies: United States and other countries that fought together against Germany and Japan during World War II

anti-Semitism: intense hatred and unfair treatment of Jewish people

collaborated: cooperated as a traitor with those who illegally control a government

concentration camps: prison camps where thousands of inmates are held under harsh conditions

couriers: people who carry messages to others

deportation: moving people from one area, usually a country, to another using force

evacuation: leaving a dangerous place to seek safety

intelligence: information gathered about a government or military force

liberation: act of freeing a nation from foreign military control

moral: related to good and evil

occupation: military control of a foreign nation

premier: title for the leader of some elected governments

refugees: people forced to flee their homes during a crisis, such as a war or natural disaster

reprisals: acts of violence carried out as punishment

sabotage: acts meant to damage or destroy property or interfere with the carrying out of certain actions

Scandinavia: region of northern Europe composed of Denmark, Norway, and Sweden; Iceland and Finland are sometimes included

shells: exploding canisters fired from large guns

Soviet Union: former nation made up of what are now Russia and 14 other countries of Eastern Europe and Central Asia

strikes: refusals to work in attempts to force employers or other authorities to agree to workers' demands

ADDITIONAL RESOURCES

Further Reading

Adams, Simon. *Under Occupation*. Mankato, Minn.: Sea-to-Sea
Publications, 2009.

Docalavich, Heather. *Denmark*. Philadelphia: Mason Crest
Publishers, 2006.

Fitzgerald, Stephanie. *Kristallnacht, The Night of Broken Glass:
Igniting the Nazi War Against Jews*. Minneapolis: Compass
Point Books, 2008.

Grant, R.G. *World War II: Europe*. Milwaukee: World Almanac
Library, 2005.

Haugen, Brenda. *Adolf Hitler: Dictator of Nazi Germany*.
Minneapolis: Compass Point Books, 2006.

Haugen, Brenda. *The Holocaust Museum*. Minneapolis:
Compass Point Books, 2008.

Levine, Ellen. *Darkness Over Denmark: The Danish Resistance and
the Rescue of the Jews*. New York: Holiday House, 2000.

Shapiro, Stephen, and Tina Forrester. *Hoodwinked: Deception
and Resistance*. Toronto: Annick Press, 2004.

Tonge, Neil. *The Holocaust*. New York: Rosen Publishing, 2009.

Internet Sites

FactHound offers a safe, fun way to find Internet sites related to this book. All of the sites on FactHound have been researched by our staff.

Here's all you do:
   Visit *www.facthound.com*
FactHound will fetch the best sites for you.

Look for more *Taking a Stand* books:

Freedom Fighter: William Wallace and Scotland's Battle for Independence
Striking Back: The Fight to End Child Labor Exploitation
United in Cause: The Sons of Liberty

SELECT BIBLIOGRAPHY

Hæstrup, Jørgen. *Secret Alliance: A Study of the Danish Resistance Movement 1940 –1945*. New York: New York University Press, 1977.

Haskew, Michael E. *The World War II Desk Reference.* New York: Grand Central Press, 2004.

Kieler, Jørgen. *Resistance Fighter.* New York: Gefen Publishing House, 2008.

Loeffler, Martha. *Boats in the Night: Knud Dyby's Story of Resistance and Rescue.* Blair, Neb.: Lur Publications, 2004.

Petrow, Richard. *The Bitter Years: The Invasion and Occupation of Denmark and Norway, April 1940–May 1945.* New York: William Morrow & Co., 1974.

Rying, Bent. *Denmark: History. Vol 2.* Copenhagen: Royal Danish Ministry of Foreign Affairs, 1981.

Sutherland, Christine. *Monica: Heroine of the Danish Resistance.* New York: Farrar, Straus, and Giroux, 1990.

Thomas, John Oram. *The Giant Killers: The Danish Resistance Movement of 1940– 1945.* New York: Taplinger Publishing Company, 1975.

Werner, Emmy E. *A Conspiracy of Decency: The Rescue of the Danish Jews During World War II.* Boulder, Colo.: Westview Press, 2002.

Wheal, Elizabeth-Anne, et al. *Encyclopedia of the Second World War.* Edison, N.J.: Castle Books, 1989.

Willmott, H.P., et al. *World War II.* New York: DK Publishing, 2004.

SOURCE NOTES

Chapter 1: Martha Loeffler, *Boats in the Night: Knud Dyby's Story of Resistance and Rescue*. Blair, Neb.: Lur Publications, 2004, p. 4.

Chapter 2: "Denmark's Faith Voiced by Envoy," *The New York Times*, June 6, 1940, p. 28.
Jørgen Kieler, *Resistance Fighter*. New York: Gefen Books, 2007, pp. 35-36.

Chapter 3: Jørgen Hæstrup, *Secret Alliance: A Study of the Danish Resistance Movement 1940–1945*. New York: New York University Press, 1976, pp. 100-101.

Chapter 4: *Resistance Fighter*, p. 72.

Chapter 5: *Secret Alliance*, p. 261.
George Axelsson, "15,000 Armed Danes Defy Nazi Tanks in Copenhagen." *The New York Times*, July 2, 1944, pp. 1, 6.

Chapter 6: Emmy E. Werner, *A Conspiracy of Decency: The Rescue of the Danish Jews During World War II*. Boulder, Colo.: Westview Press, 2002, p. 143.

INDEX

ABOUT THE AUTHOR

Michael Burgan is a freelance writer of books for children and adults. A history graduate of the University of Connecticut, he has written more than 200 fiction and nonfiction children's books. For adult audiences he has written news articles, essays, and plays. Michael Burgan is a recipient of an Educational Press Association of America award.